LUTON LIBRARIES

Renewals, online accounts, catalogue searches, eBooks and other online services:
www.lutonlibraries.co.uk

Renewals: 01582 547413

Luton Culture

WHY DO I SWEAT?

BY Emilie Dufresne

BookLife PUBLISHING

©2019
BookLife Publishing Ltd.
King's Lynn
Norfolk PE30 4LS

All rights reserved.
Printed in Malaysia.

A catalogue record for this book is available from the British Library.

ISBN: 978-1-78637-568-1

Written by:
Emilie Dufresne

Edited by:
John Wood

Designed by:
Danielle Rippengill

All facts, statistics, web addresses and URLs in this book were verified as valid and accurate at time of writing. No responsibility for any changes to external websites or references can be accepted by either the author or publisher.

Image Credits

All images are courtesy of Shutterstock.com, unless otherwise specified. With thanks to Getty Images, Thinkstock Photo and iStockphoto. Front Cover & 1 – Dmitry Natashin, Nadzin, Bukavik, BigMouse, MaryValery. Images used on every spread – Nadzin, TheFarAwayKingdom. 2 – svtdesign, Anna Violet. 4-7 – Iconic Bestiari. 8 – Irina Shatilova, Kanitta Kuha, VectorKnight. 9 – Iconic Bestiary. 10 & 11 – I LOVE YOU. 12 – Bukavik, BigMouse, MaryValery. 13 – Finevector. 14 – Pogorelova Olga, Vector Studio, BlueRingMedia. 15 – svtdesign. 16 & 17 – Iconic Bestiary. 17 – maglyvi. 18 & 19 – svtdesign, Anna Violet. 20 – svtdesign. 21 – Mountain Brothers, 10topvector, Olga1818. 22 – PixMarket. 23 – Iconic Bestiary.

CONTENTS

PAGE 4   **Are You Feeling Warm?**

PAGE 6   **Sweat It Out…**

PAGE 8   **Keep It Level**

PAGE 10   **Where Do We Sweat?**

PAGE 12   **Exercise**

PAGE 14   **Feeling Feverish?**

PAGE 16   **Cold Sweats**

PAGE 18   **Fuzzy Bodies**

PAGE 20   **Smelly Sweat**

PAGE 22   **Sweat Stats**

PAGE 24   **Glossary and Index**

*Words that look like **this** can be found in the glossary on page 24.*

Are You Feeling Warm?

Have you ever got a bit warm and noticed your body getting sticky and wet in certain places?

Phew!

We can sweat for lots of different reasons. Sometimes it is because of the temperature. Sometimes we sweat as a reaction to our emotions.

Being nervous or scared can make us sweat.

Sweaty Forehead

Sweat It Out...

We need to sweat in order to keep our bodies at the right temperature. If our bodies get too warm, sweating helps us cool down.

Our bodies should be around 37 degrees Celsius (°C).

As we sweat, our skin becomes wet with **liquid**. This liquid turns into a **vapour** as it leaves our skin. This process is called evaporation (SAY: EE-VAP-OR-AY-SHUN).

VAPOUR

VAPOUR

As this happens, our skin is cooled.

Keep It Level

Sweating is an example of homeostasis **(SAY: HOME-EE-OH-STAY-SIS)**. Homeostasis is the method our bodies use to keep lots of different things at the right levels.

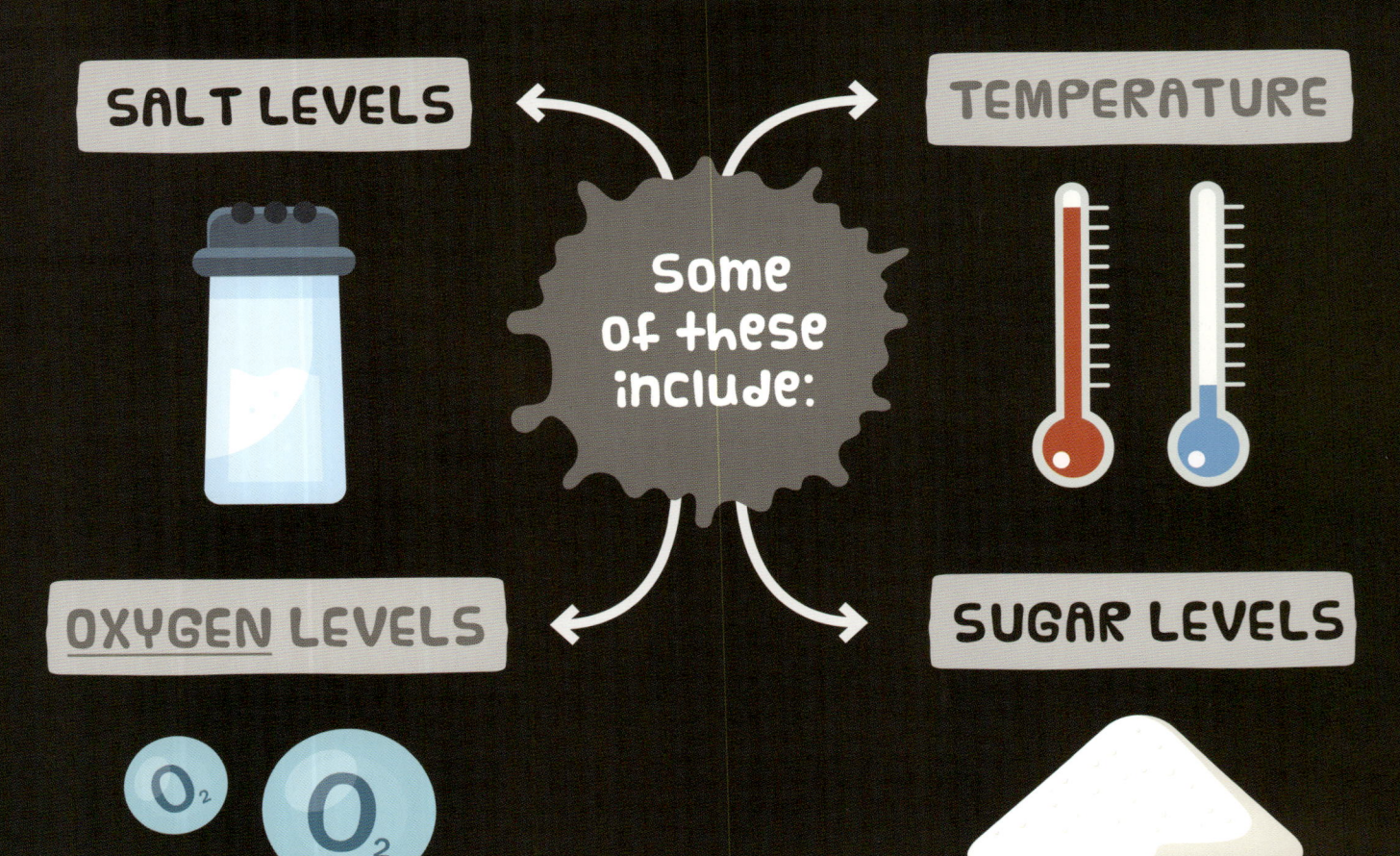

Some of these include:

- SALT LEVELS
- TEMPERATURE
- OXYGEN LEVELS
- SUGAR LEVELS

If we get cold, we shiver to warm up.

If the environment changes around us, homeostasis makes sure that it won't affect our bodies on the inside. For example, if we get hot, we sweat to cool down.

Where Do We Sweat?

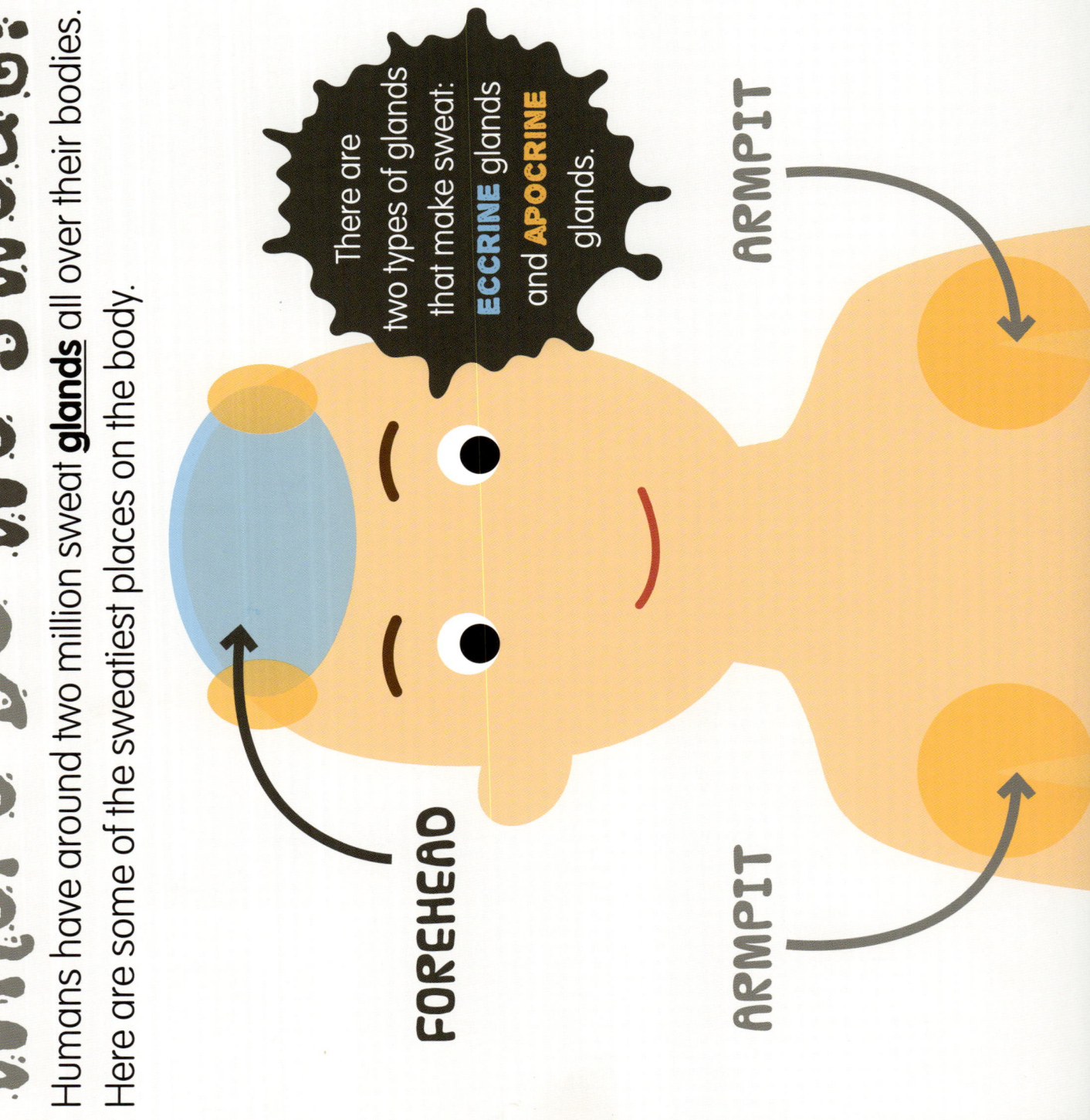

Humans have around two million sweat **glands** all over their bodies. Here are some of the sweatiest places on the body.

There are two types of glands that make sweat: **ECCRINE** glands and **APOCRINE** glands.

FOREHEAD

ARMPIT

ARMPIT

PALM

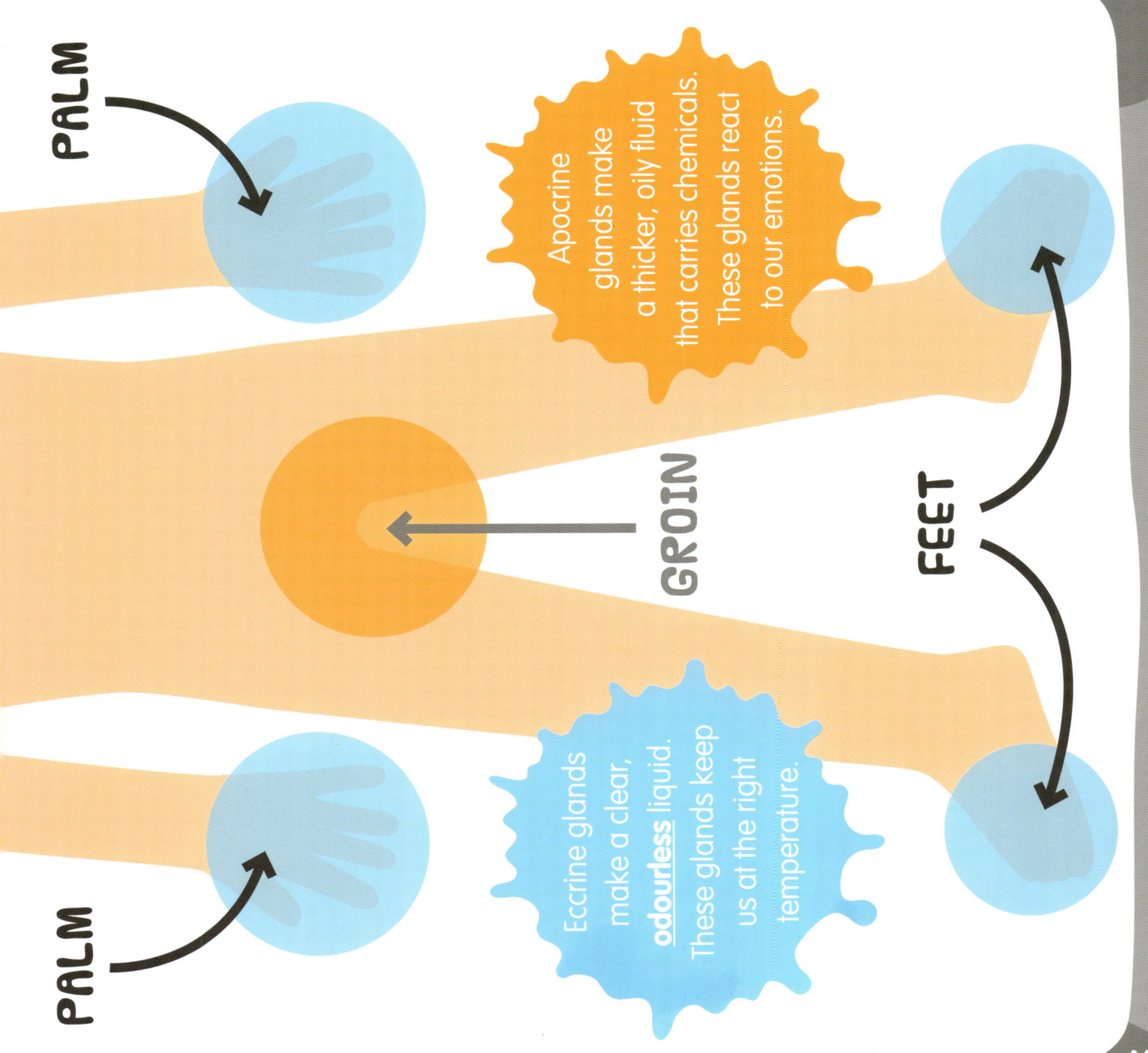

Apocrine glands make a thicker, oily fluid that carries chemicals. These glands react to our emotions.

GROIN

FEET

Eccrine glands make a clear, **odourless** liquid. These glands keep us at the right temperature.

PALM

exercise

When we exercise, we are more likely to sweat. This is because exercise raises our body temperature. We lose lots of **minerals** when we sweat.

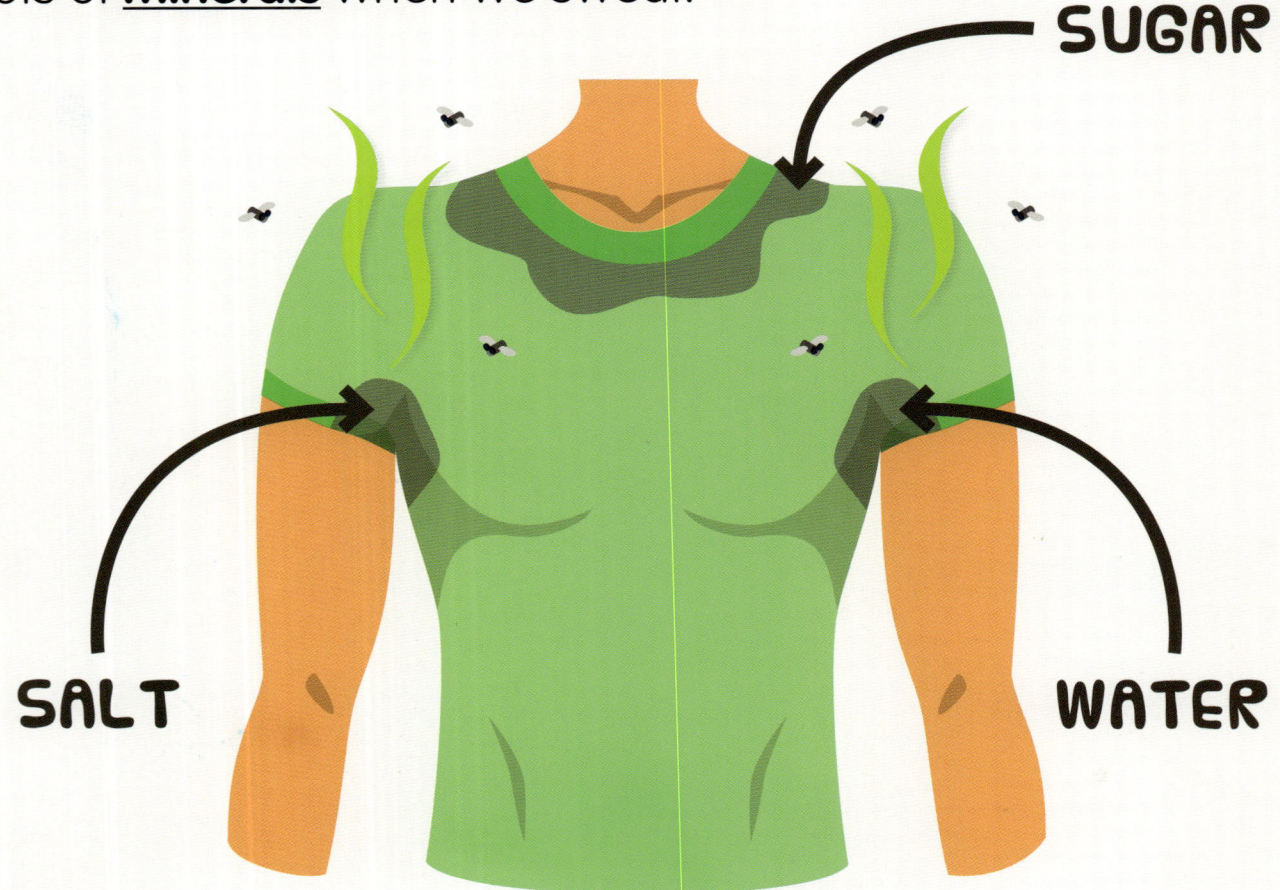

SUGAR

SALT

WATER

We have to drink lots of water when we exercise because we lose so much through sweating.

GLUG! GLUG! GLUG!

Feeling Feverish?

Sometimes when we get ill or sick, we might get a high temperature. This might make us sweat. These illnesses could be:

Coughs and Colds

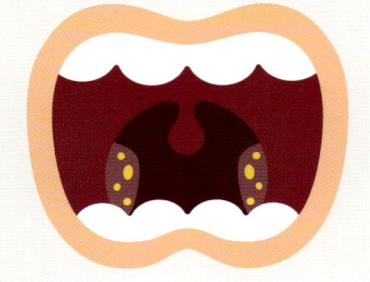

Tonsillitis

Ear Infections

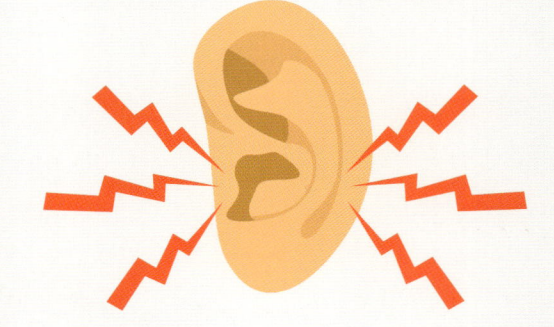

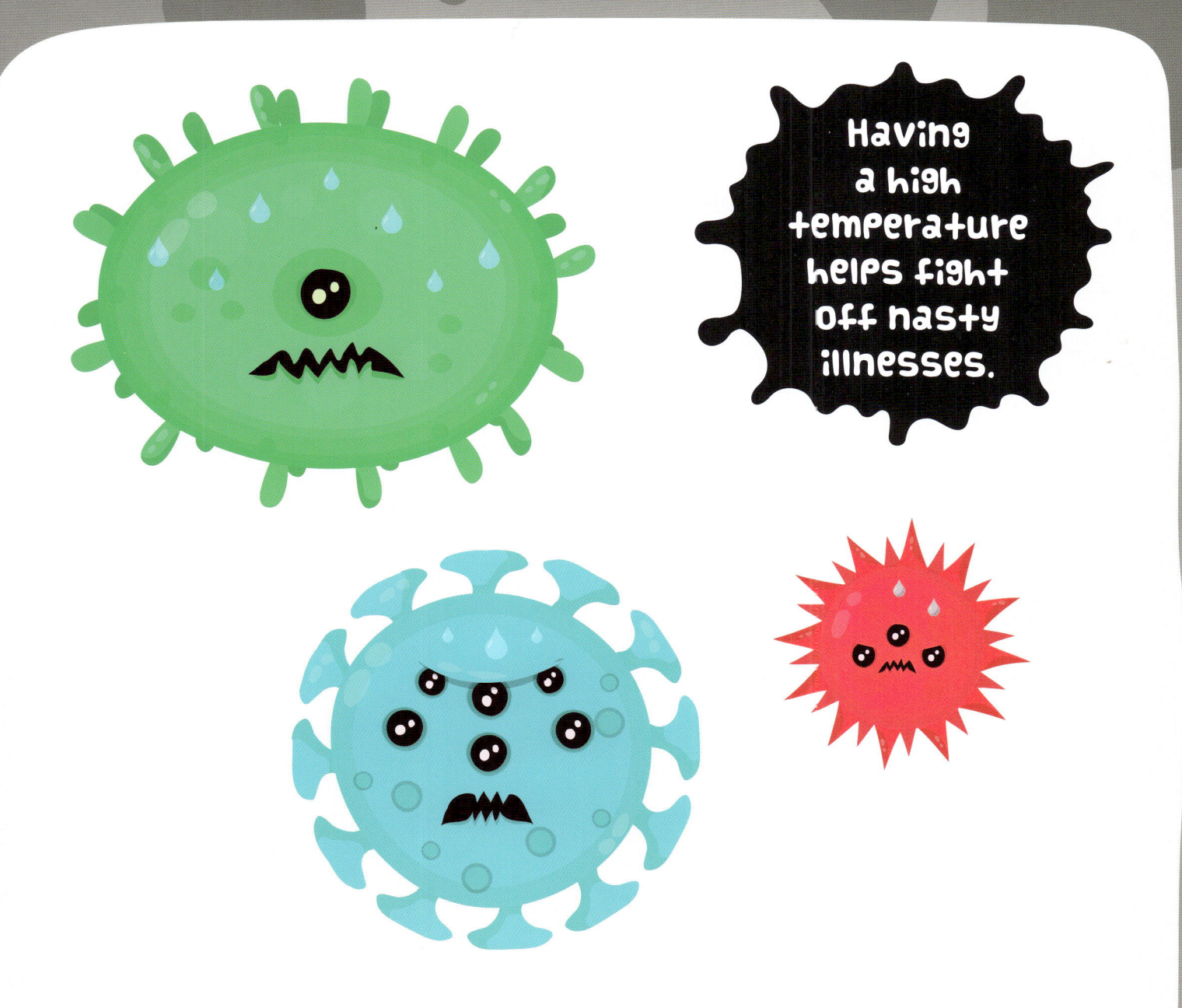

Having a high temperature helps fight off nasty illnesses.

Having a high temperature and sweating is one way our body protects us. Lots of **bacteria** and **viruses** that cause illnesses can't survive in very warm bodies.

Cold Sweats

Cold sweats are different to normal sweating. Instead of sweating because your body is too hot, cold sweats are a reaction to other things.

You can get cold sweats for lots of reasons, such as being shocked or having a sudden fright. These can make your hands and feet clammy.

BOO!

Fuzzy Bodies

Did you know that you have tiny hairs that cover most of your body? These are vellus hairs and they help our bodies stay at the right temperature.

These hairs help us when we are hot.

VELLUS HAIR

When we are hot, our sweat coats the vellus hairs. The hairs help the sweat evaporate, letting us cool down.

VAPOUR

SWEAT

VELLUS HAIR

Smelly Sweat

Sometimes when we sweat, things can get a little bit pongy. But it isn't our sweat that smells. It's the bacteria breaking down our sweat that makes us stink!

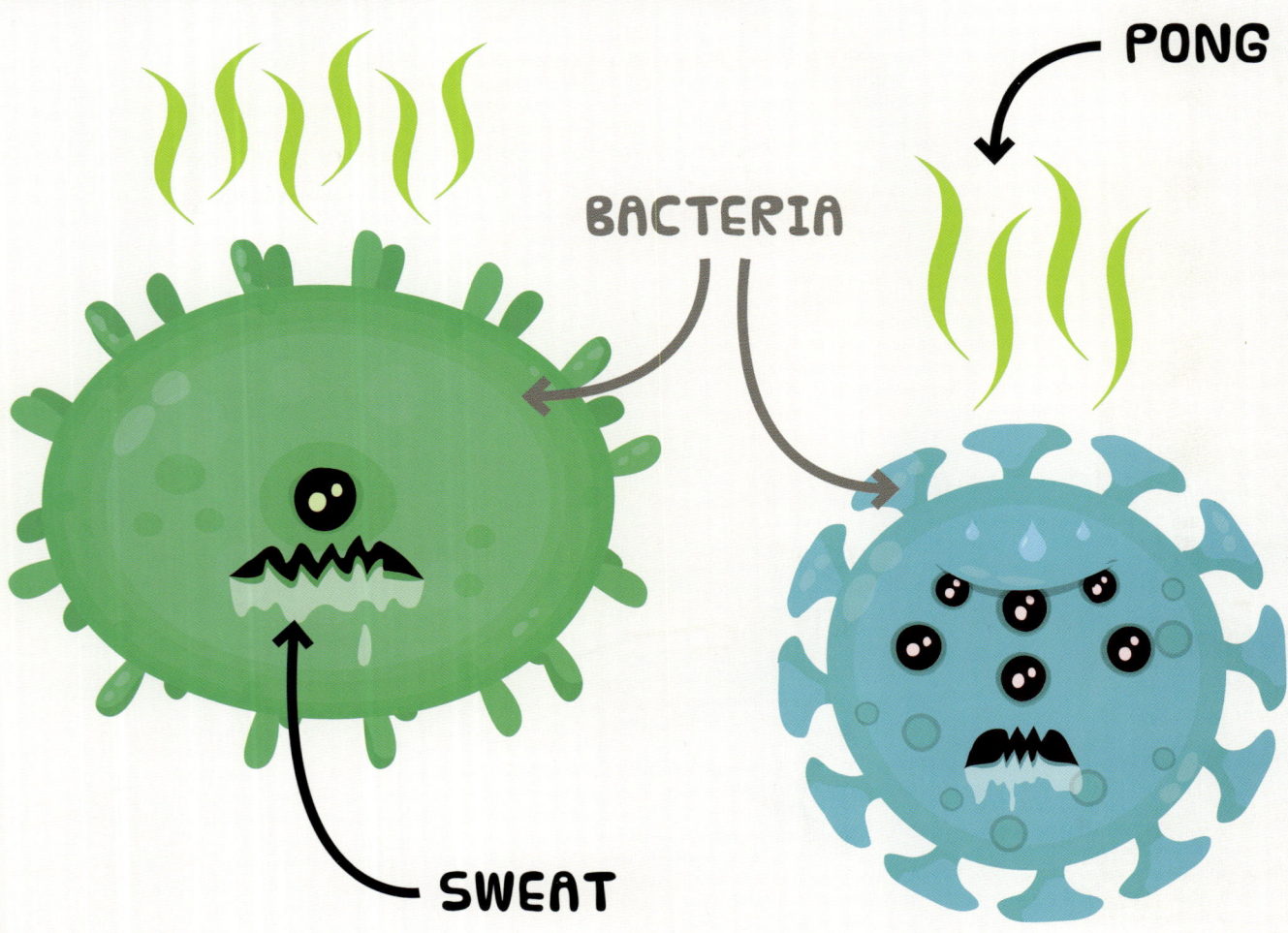

PONG

BACTERIA

SWEAT

RED MEAT →

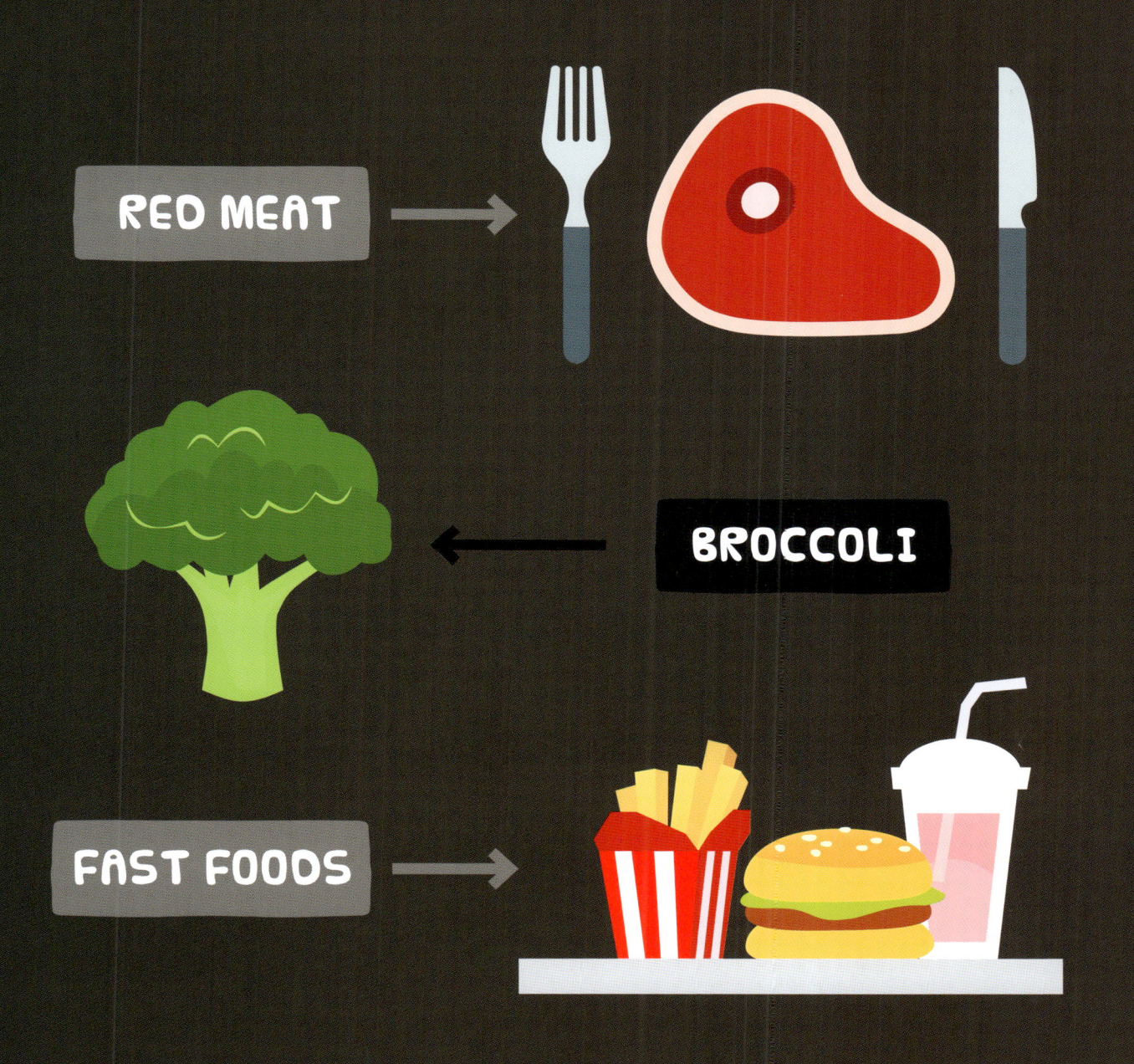

← BROCCOLI

FAST FOODS →

It is thought that some foods can make our sweat smell more than others. If you eat a lot of these foods, you might be more whiffy than usual.

Sweat Stats

Did you know that hippos have red sweat?
It helps protect their skin in the heat by acting like sun cream.

The sweat also kills harmful bacteria on their skin.

The **average** person will sweat around 183 litres a year. That's about a whole bath full of sweat!

The maximum amount of sweat a person can produce in a day is 14 litres!

Glossary

average — the typical and usual; not outside the ordinary

bacteria — microscopic living things that can cause diseases

glands — a type of organ in the body that produces chemicals

liquid — a material that flows, such as water

minerals — important things that plants, animals or humans need to grow

odourless — to have no detectable smell

oxygen — a natural gas that living things need in order to survive

vapour — tiny parts of a solid or liquid that float in the air as a gas, such as mist or steam

viruses — tiny living things that live inside other things and make them ill

Index

bacteria 15, 20, 22
body 4, 6, 8–12, 15–16, 18
emotions 5, 11
exercise 12–13
hair 18–19
salt 8, 12
sugar 8, 12
temperature 5–6, 8, 11–12, 14–15, 18
vapour 7, 19
warm 4, 6, 9, 15